ALFA ROMEO
SPIDER

ALFA ROMEO SPIDER

David Sparrow and Adrienne Kessel

First published in Great Britain in 1995
by Osprey, an imprint of Reed Consumer
Books Limited, Michelin House,
81 Fulham Road, London SW3 6RB and
Auckland, Melbourne, Singapore and Toronto.

ISBN 1 85532 523 3

Editor Simon McAuslane
Page design Paul Kime/Ward Peacock
Partnership

Printed in Hong Kong

Half title
*The Alfa Romeo trademark consists of
the crest of the city of Milan and the
Visconti family crest. The snake-dragon
represented the virtues of military
endeavour: loyalty, vigilance and valour.
It devours the family's enemies*

Title page
*Fourth series Spider, see page 78. The
rear of the car owes a debt of gratitude
to the Alfa Romeo 164. The boot-top
spoiler is gone, the rear bumper matches
that at the front, wraparound in style
and body-coloured. The lighting clusters
imply a complete horizontal strip that
has been intruded into by the licence
plate recess. The Alfa Romeo badge sits
horizontally, centrally placed on top of
the bootlid*

Right
*Second series: see page 58. There was a
small but important market for the right
hand drive version, mainly for Great
Britain. In 1968, three hundred right
hand drive Spiders were imported. Right
hand drives continued to be imported
until the beginning of 1975, when
production gradually petered out - for a
little while*

For a catalogue of all books published by Osprey Automotive
please write to:

**The Marketing Department, Reed Consumer Books,
1st Floor, Michelin House, 81 Fulham Road, London SW3 6RB**

Contents

Introduction

Societa Anonima Lomarda Fabbrica Automobili was founded in 1910 by Ugo Stella, after the liquidation of the Darracq assembly plant at Portello, where he had been managing director. Despite a healthy following in France, Darracqs had proved unequal to the task on Italian roads, and the exported parts for assembly had not always been up to scratch.

Stella appreciated that a successful indigenous Italian car would need to be a tough, competent animal of exemplary design, with all the best qualities of both workhorse and thoroughbred racer. As his chief designer he chose Guisseppe Merosi, who worked locally in Milan at the time for Bianchi. Originally a building surveyor by trade, Merosi's experience of car design included time at Merchand, Lentz and, most significantly, a year in Fiat's racing car design department in Turin. The first ALFA, a 24hp 4.1 litre four-cylinder car which could reach more than 60mph, was a splendidly grand open tourer, light in weight but robustly built for Italian conditions.

While the new motor car from Milan was starting to make a name for itself, elsewhere in the Lombardian capital Nicola Romeo was in the process of setting up his own manufacturing company, making mining machinery, including a portable compressed air plant. Commercial success soon followed, the company increasing twelve-fold in the space of only six months at one point. Romeo was a hard working and dedicated man; he had a degree in electrical engineering and experience of working in many European countries. At the end of 1915 he bought ALFA from its shareholders, and car production ceased to make way for the necessities of war, such as aircraft engines and compressors, as well as general engineering products, including ploughs and tractors.

The Alfa Spider, meaning of course the 1966 Duetto and subsequent versions, rather than any earlier open-topped treatment, became one of the benchmarks of style for the generation whose lot it was, for good or ill, to be young in the sixties. Traditional boundaries were being pushed to the limits, post-war conventions had already been challenged. 'Italian' spelled style: an accessible European style with a hint of American braggadocio about it. Dustin Hoffman driving a Duetto in the film The Graduate *gave the Alfa's publicity a welcome boost*

Romeo liked motor cars; the idea of a thoroughly Milanese motor car held great appeal to him. The Great War was over. The practical exigences it had placed on his business for four years were lifted. It was time for the Portello factory to start thinking again about motor cars – cars that henceforth would bear the name Alfa Romeo.

In 1920, Merosi began work on designing a new car for a new decade; the RL was unveiled in Milan the following year. It proved itself a popular production car, as well as providing the company with racing success in the Targa Florio. Merosi was replaced as designer in 1926 by Fiat's Vittorio Jano. Throughout the twenties and thirties the redesigned six-cylinder descendants of the RL and their eight-cylinder counterparts were clothed by a number of coachbuilding 'names'; Touring and

Times change, and the children of the sixties have matured. The Alfa Spider has been in production for more than a quarter of a century, encompassing on its way four distinct series, each with its own version of the Spider style, each with its own aficionados. The original Duetto, the Kamm-tailed version, the aerodynamica, and the current and last series introduced in 1990, which pleased so many 'Alfisti', who felt that it signified a return to real Alfa Spider style. The history of Alfa the company spans more than eighty years, which can be divided into three: the pre-war years - elegant coachbuilt cars with a racing pedigree; from the war to the sixties - a gradual move towards smaller, more economic cars and mass production; and from the mid-sixties to the present day - the age of the Spider

Castagna, Zagato and Farina, as well as offerings from Alfa themselves. Spanish engineer Wilfredo Ricart took the design helm from 1940 although Italy's entry into the war ensured that his designs didn't get much further than drawing board or prototype stage. Nicola Romeo died on 15 August 1938. Cars were still produced at Portello during the war years, albeit at a trickle. However, the devastation caused by the Allied bombing made it impossible to contemplate putting any new designs into production with any hope of economic success, and so the pre-war cars enjoyed an Indian, and several Italian, summers. The Portello factory had been bombed for the first time on St Valentine's Day 1943, again in August that year and one more in October 1944, which makes the speed of the company's recovery - both in production and on the track - all the more remarkable.

The days of the luxury touring cars were over; post-war austerity demanded something more practical. Under Orazio Satta, now Alfa's chief designer, a four-cylinder 1884 engine was developed, and the 1900 range was born. This was the first car produced in any volume by Alfa Romeo; during its eight years in production, variously styled bodies from the major coachbuilders were offered, as well as the factory version. 1029 Pinin Farina-designed cabriolets were built, all of them during 1952. Six years later, Alfa Romeo commissioned Touring to produce a Spider based on the Berlina 2000 as a replacement. The front of this Spider bears a family resemblance to the Giulietta, although the rest of the styling is more grand, as befits the larger scale of the car; a second cousin maybe, but family for certain. The four-cylinder 2000 was replaced with the six-cylinder 2600 from 1962. Altogether, just under 6000 cars were built by Touring before production ceased in 1965.

1954 saw Alfa Romeo in state ownership, and on the threshold of a period as a major volume manufacturer. Enter the 'Good Idea' – the state lottery-assisted funding of a new mass-produced car, the Giulietta range. The prizes were to be Giuliettas, of course. The lottery was held, the draw was made, but no prizes had been built. Bertone was commissioned to produce some cars quickly, in order to defuse what threatened to be an ugly situation. This coupé version continued to be made by Bertone, with Alfa themselves producing the saloon and Pinin Farina the Giulietta Spider version from 1955. The cars were fitted with a four-cylinder 1290cc engine which was capable of 160km/h. A more powerful Veloce version was produced the following year, which had a top speed of 180km/h. The Giulietta range evolved into the Giulias in 1962. The styling of the new cars was largely unchanged. The Giulia 1600 was joined in 1965 by a Veloce version, both ceasing production in 1965.

In 1952 the 'Disco Volante' (flying Saucer), appeared. A prototype sports-car racer, its mechanicals were derived from the 1900 and the body came courtesy of Touring. The Disco Volante project was inspired by Alfa themselves with the aim of encouraging research and development of competition cars in general, and aerodynamic applications in particular.

At the Turin Motor Show of 1956, a Pinin Farina-designed car was shown that introduced for the first time some of the styling characteristics of the Alfa Spider. This was the Super Flow, (see page 95) a concept car with American-style back fins, cut-away front wheel arches, bonnet-length transparent plastic 'wings', and the evocative sculptured side lines of the Spider that would appear ten years later. At the Paris Motor Show in the same year, the Super Flow II made its debut. It was less futuristic-looking than its predecessor; plastic coverings to the headlamps had evolved from those wings, the nose was more rounded and the front wheels less bare. The Super Flow cars bore more than a passing resemblance to the Ferarri Super Fast which was shown at the Paris Salon in the same year.

Three years later, in 1959, another unique Pinin Farina design was shown, at Geneva this time. The Spider Super Sport is a beautiful evolutionary stage, the penultimate step on Pinin Farina's style journey towards the Duetto Spider. The last step appeared at Turin in 1961; the Giulietta Spider Speciale.

And so, by the start of 1966, the scene was set for something new in open-topped motoring from Alfa Romeo. It would be a story with four chapters, spanning a quarter of a century; and be a narrative all about a universally recognisable shape.

History

Alfa themselves clothed this 8C 2900, although similar creations were available from the styling houses of both Farina and Touring. The chassis was available in both short and long wheelbase versions. The former was used successfully for the competition cars which won the Mille Miglia in 1938 and 1947. The longer wheelbase was the basis for the elegantly coachbuilt road-going cars which were first presented at the Paris Salon in 1935

The Geneva Motor Show, which took place on 10 March 1966, was the venue for the presentation of the new Alfa Romeo Spider. The car turned out to be Pininfarina's swansong; he died less than a month after the car's launch. Future offerings from the house of Pininfarina would bear the new form of the family surname, which he had succeeded in changing earlier that year.

At its debut, the new Alfa had no name, save the unimaginative 'Spider 1600' tag from the Giulia's 1570cc engine. With one of those flashes of inspiration that have so often dogged automotive marketing, Alfa decided to organise a 'name the baby' competition, entry forms available at your local dealer, no purchase necessary. The prize was a Spider, and naturally enough, there were thousands of entries from Italy and beyond. The name chosen was 'Duetto'. The winner's name was duly drawn, and his prize presented. But there was a problem; the name 'Duetto' already belonged to an Italian biscuit manufacturer. And so the 'Duetto' tag was dropped, indeed it was never really taken up as an official title. It had, in any case, been thought weak and unimaginative by many, and the Romeo/Giulia play on words rather laboured, although the 'car-built-for-two' allusion held some appeal.

The Spider already had an in-house nickname, 'Osso di Seppia' (cuttlefish bone), from its novel shape, and this unofficial name stuck, at least in the countries where cuttlefish, and the shape of their bones, form a part of everyday life. To English-speakers, this first shape became known as the boat-tailed Spider. At the start of 1968, Alfa Romeo brought out a more powerful version, called the 1750 Spider Veloce as per their normal convention, which was fitted with a 1779cc engine. In the summer of the same year, the Spider was also fitted with a 1290cc engine similar to that of the Giulietta, this version becoming known as the Spider 1300 Junior. There were minor cosmetic modifications for this less expensive Spider, the most obvious being the lack of perspex cowling over the headlamps.

Despite the popularity of the shape of the original Spider with both the motoring press and the public, and the origin of its nickname from that shape, there were those at Alfa Romeo who felt that the rear end

would benefit from reworking, making it less stylised and more aerodynamic. The rear was in effect 'chopped' in the style of a Kamm tail, which resulted in a shorter car with a more conventional shape and a larger luggage space in the boot. The rear light clusters were modernised too. At the front end, the shield device was flattened and widened slightly. Both the 1750 Spider Veloce and the 1300 Junior were produced in this second series of Spiders from 1969 onwards.

In 1971, Alfa Romeo presented its 2000 range, developed from the 1750 with the help of experience gained in the competition field. The

Above

The SS Corsa Spider, styled by Touring Superleggera is a rare beast; only eight were built, four each in 1939 and 1940. They notched up 1st, 2nd and 4th in the Tobruk to Tripoli competition in 1939, plus second place in the following year's Mille Miglia, three others gaining top ten places too. The car was built on the 6C 2500 Sport chassis; the lines are aerodynamic, the profile sculptured

Left

The much-respected 1900 series represented a significant step on Alfa's road to volume production. This was the first car from the company of monocoque construction, designed by Alessio, paving the way, both in engineering, production and styling, for the Giulietta series. In line with this approach, the Farina-styled cabriolet has an airy feeling of fun, sporty motoring for all. The cars were sturdy and reliable, and much sought-after

2000 Spider Veloce remained in production for eleven years, and was a popular version with highly regarded performance. Meanwhile, in 1972, the Spider Junior 1600 made its debut (fitted with the same engine as the original Duetto) to which in performance, if not in rear styling, it was almost identical.

The early eighties were a time of change. Seventies style was of a kind which dates very quickly, and there were those who felt that the new-style Spider of 1983 was an example of change for change's sake, money for God's sake. All of which is not to portray the new Spider as a fashion victim; Pininfarina had presented a styling exercise almost a decade earlier on which its aerodynamic properties were clearly based. The most obvious elemental change was the addition of front and rear spoilers, painted metal at the front and black synthetic material at the rear. Bumpers became more integrated with the body shape, and the grille/badge partnership became more stylised. Perspex cowlings disappeared completely. The interior was also overhauled. This third series became known as 'aerodynamica'. Following on from the previous models, there were two versions; the 1.6 and the 2.0.

In 1986 a top-of-the-range Spider with sporting aspirations made its debut – the Quadrifoglio Verde. It had extra side skirts and modified spoilers; the specification was extensive, with a high price tag to match.

The fourth and final version of the Spider was unveiled in 1990, the eightieth anniversary of the existence of Alfa. The engines utilised were the same as before: 1.6 and 2.0 versions. The major styling changes were the loss of the spoilers, with an altogether lighter and softer feel to both the front and rear. The interior appointment and finishing were tidied and refined.

There will not be another Alfa Romeo Spider of the same genre as these four versions. 1995 brought a very different Spider, although Pininfarina styling was still in evidence, as was the influence of Alfa Romeo's many years in the design and production of sporting cars.

In 1958, the 2000 Spider, designed by Touring and built on the chassis of the Berlina 2000, replaced the 1900. The 2600 Spider with its six-cylinder 2584cc engine, replaced the 2000 in 1962. The car was luxurious in terms of interior specification and trim, with a horizontal speedometer, an unusual styling cue at that time. There is a strong exterior resemblance to the Giulietta. This Spider remained in production for seven years

Above

The forerunner of the Duetto, and precursor of all the Spider versions that were to follow; the Giulietta. The beginnings of the Giulietta series marked Alfa's true arrival as a force to be reckoned with in the mass-production market. When the new Farina-designed Spider was introduced, comparison with the much loved Giulietta was inevitable. Journalists and marque enthusiasts were divided, some judging the Duetto a worthy successor, others vehement in their criticism of the 'young upstart' with its radical styling

Right

The Giulia Spider is largely identical in looks to the Giulietta version. The 'air-scoop' on the bonnet isn't there at all of course, it's a bulge to provide the extra height required in the engine compartment to accommodate the larger 1600 power unit. Over 10,000 Giulia Spiders were constructed in all, with bodies supplied by Farina

Above

The Giulia TI, which had been introduced in June '62 provided the 1570cc engine which powered the Duetto. A GT Veloce version of the Giulia was unveiled alongside the Duetto at the Geneva Motor Show of 1966. Facelifts aside, the Giulia continued in production in various guises right up to 1976

Above right

Alfa's press information around the time of the Duetto's launch included some indication of the competition, as Alfa saw it, in the marketplace. Italian rivalry included the Fiat 1500 and 1600 cabriolets, which had the leading edge on price. Even the 3.8 E-type Jaguar cost just 3.7% more than the Alfa, with no comparison in performance capabilities. Less than six months after the launch, Pininfarina themselves began producing the Fiat 124 Sport Spider, reckoned to be the Alfa's most serious rival for the affections of the public

Right

The Alfa Romeo logo has evolved in several stages during the eighty-plus years of the company's existence. The two major elements, the red cross of the City of Milan, and the man-eating snake from the Visconti crest have remained. When the Duetto was introduced, the logo sported a laurel crown surround, in celebration of Alfa's World Championship victory in 1925. From 1972, the crown was represented by two narrow circles, the word 'Milano' was dropped to take account of Alfa's plants further afield, and the crowned snake and his prey were stylised

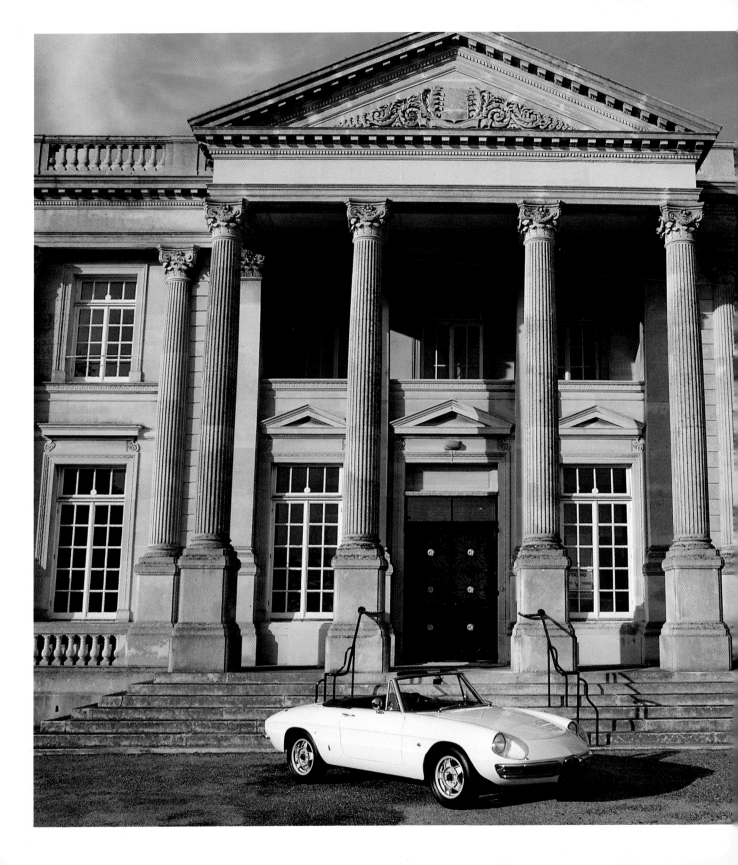

Osso di Seppia

Above

Although the name for the new car was chosen by means of a world-wide competition, someone at Alfa must have made the decision that 'Duetto' was the best suggestion. The name of triumphant Guidobaldi Trionfi was drawn from all the 'Duetto' supporters. Perhaps it was thought the name least likely to offend, for, quite apart from a whole host of girl's names in the Giulietta/Giulia tradition, among the suggestions put forward were Shakespeare, Stalin, Pizza and Eidelweiss

Left

It was the naturally uncontrived nickname for the car that stuck though, and when it was decided not to take up the 'Duetto' option for reasons of legality, 'Osso di Seppia' (cuttle-fish bone) it became, strictly unofficially. The 'boat-tail' tag given to the Duetto in English speaking countries serves more to distinguish the first cars from the later Kamm-tailed version than to describe the whole shape

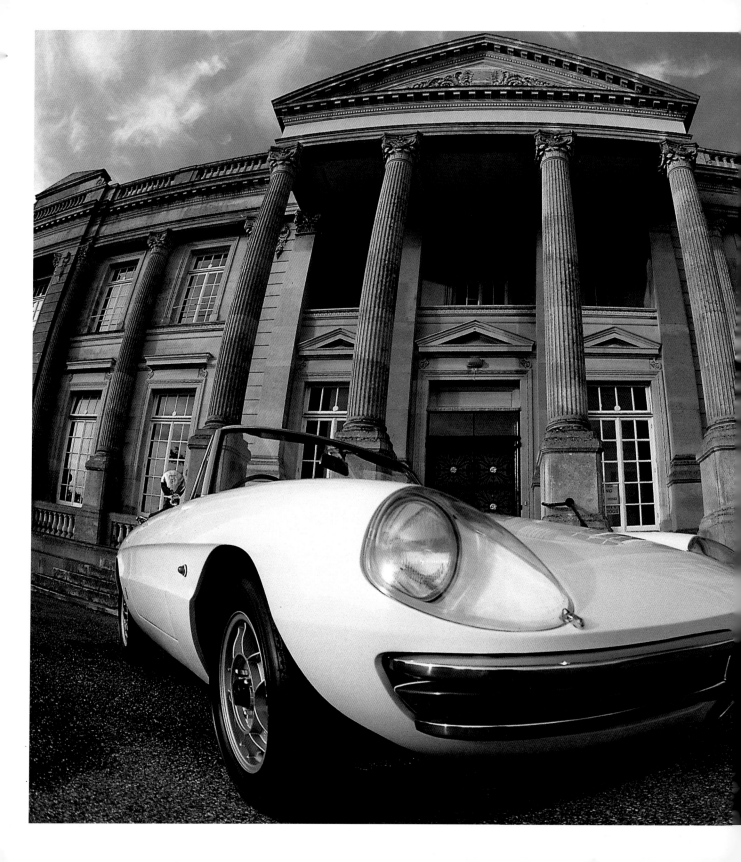

Above

The characteristic perspex-covered headlamps are a Pininfarina speciality, appearing on the Ferraris too. The Super Flow concept car had been equipped with entire bonnet length wing sections of perspex. The Spider's headlamp covers were easily removable; when driving on dipped lights at night in bad weather it was necessary to remove them for better light projection – the covers when wet serving to scatter the light rather than concentrate it

Left and overleaf

Certainly reaction to the Spider's innovative shape were mixed. Road & Track found almost no-one in their offices who preferred the shape to the Giulia. "A contrived design with meaningless styling gimmicks" and "compact, and rather ugly," were two of the harsher comments. But many fortunate enough to get a Spider on loan for test driving admitted that they grew more fond of the shape the more they saw of it. Many Spider owners are loyal to the marque and the model. Sixties swinging singles became seventies family saloon owners: and nineties empty nests mean that some can look forward to Spider ownership the second time around

Above
The boat-tailed rear end incorporates the rear light cluster within its shape. The outer edge of the cluster reflects the shape of the tapered end of the side scallop, thus maintaining styling integrity

Right
The most distinctive styling feature of the Spider was the full length scalloped shape along the side from the top of the front wheel arch to the rear light cluster. Along with the slightly snout-shaped front end, it gives an overall sporting elan to the car when it is in motion

Above
As well as Alfa's famous red colour, the Spider of 1966 was available in a choice of white, ivory, graphite, black, light blue or dark blue. The only available colour for the interior, and for the hood, was black

Right
The Duetto bodyshells were constructed at the Pininfarina factory in Turin. They were taken to the Alfa factory at Arese by road to be mated with their mechanical parts before being finished, tested and delivered

Above

One advantage of the Duetto over other sports cars was the relatively soft and comfortable ride. Rear seat accommodation was suitable only for the very short or very young, and even then only for short distances. Front seat space was good, although taller drivers sometimes had problems compromising the seat position for comfortable reach of both the pedals and the hand controls. There seems to be a definite Latin predisposition toward short legs and long arms – when it comes to driving position, not physiologically you understand

Right

Early cars had the wing mirror fitted some way forward of the windscreen, where it was almost impossible to adjust from the driver's seat. In this position though, it did at least fall naturally within the driver's field of vision. Later, the mirror was moved to the door, level with the quarterlight. Here it was easy to adjust, but was no longer in the driver's immediate field of view, so a deliberate turn of the head was needed. Very much a case of swings and roundabouts, as with so much of automotive design. A handsome enough mirror though, wherever positioned

Above

Instrumentation was clear and concise, with large speedo and rev counter in a binnacle centred behind the wheel. Smaller oil, water and petrol gauges sit in the centre, over a 'Pininfarina' scripted plate which is removed to fit a radio. There is an air vent at each end of the dash, and a lockable glovebox within the body-coloured panel in a style reminiscent of the VW Beetle

Left

Motor were impressed with the performance of their test Spider: "…its handling is really outstanding - the Duetto is a supremely 'chuckable' car…Bumpy surfaces do not deflect the Duetto very much during hard cornering, and unlike quite a few modern sportscars, it runs arrow-straight at high speeds"

Above

The Spider's elegant front shape could be vulnerable; more than one test car was returned by a shamefaced journo to Alfa with a restyled nose. (One might call it the compact version.) More often than not the damage was done while the car was parked, by someone else. The American magazine Car & Driver believed the Alfa had "a pristine life expectancy of about three minutes in any supermarket parking lot"

Left

The original hubcaps came in for a lot of criticism. In the context of the striking, modernistic styling of the car generally, they were thought too conservative and boring. The design was modified on later models; there are beautiful Spiders accurately restored whose original hubcaps only come out on concours occasions

Above
By 1968, the Alfa Romeo Spider had won a place in many hearts. It was rapidly coming to represent a certain Italian style; it was a car for the sunshine, for sharing, a car built for two. Hood down, it was a car where speed was secondary to the sheer pleasure of driving

Right
Back in Giulietta/Giulia days, Alfa Romeo had been very much in the habit of producing a higher-powered version of their cars, marketed alongside the original. In 1968, the Veloce version of the Spider was unveiled at the Brussels Motor Show. This was the 1750 Spider Veloce, which was capable of a top speed of 190km/h – 5km/h faster than its stablemate

Above

The hubcaps of the earliest Siders were variously described as 'antiquated', 'ugly', and 'out of character'. This replacement was more in step with the rest of the design

Left

1968 1750. A problem facing the British Spider owner: how to reconcile that huge number plate that the law requires with the front of a car that cries out out for those tiny Italian ones. The self-adhesive is a disagreeable compromise

Overleaf

Comparing the Spider with other cars in its class, the Road Test journalist enthused: 'for the driver who wants an open two-seater of a distinctly sporty and prestige nature, and who appreciates really fine handling and long-distance cruising ability…it is a good choice for the money.' (Photographs by Andrew Morland)

Junior

One of the major criticisms directed at the Alfa Spider had been its price. So, in the summer of 1968, a less expensive version, called the 1300 Junior, was launched. It was fitted with a version of the 1290cc engine, and its top speed was 170km/h

The most immediately obvious difference in the styling of the 1300 Junior was the absence of the Perspex headlamp covers. The side indicator repeaters moved forward in front of the wheel arch, and the hubcaps were slightly redesigned. Inside, the steering wheel had two spokes instead of three

Above

The major difference between the Junior and its two counterparts though, was price. The cost of a Junior was only three-quarters that of the 1750. Naturally, performance was down, but not ridiculously so. The Junior represented good value for money, and brought Spider motoring within the range of the less affluent, usually younger buyer

Left

In total, 6325 1600 Duettos were built, between 1966 and 1968. Of the 1750 Veloce version, 8722 cars were made, between 1967 and 1971, approximately half of these being boat-tailed Spiders and the remainder Kamm-tailed. Half of the Veloce production was destined for the American market. 7237 1300 Juniors were made, in a decade of production from 1968, of which no more than one-third were of the boat-tailed variety

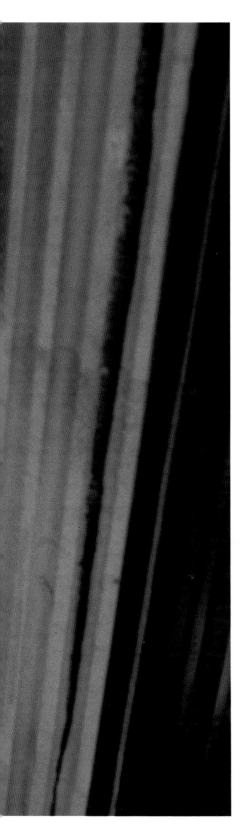

Above
Italian plates look best on a Spider; discreet and small enough not to overbalance the important front end symmetry. Black style French plates suit too, and the Americans have a degree of flexibility with theirs which often makes aesthetes of the Old World jealous. German offerings start to get awkward, while modern British ones contrive to ruin the effect at both ends

Left
The Spider's hood was remarkable for being easy to manage. Unlike some other open-tops, there were no unwieldy folding operations to be overcome. The hood could be raised and lowered by the driver, from his seat, without contortions

Left

 Owners and testers complimented the Spider for its lack of draughts and the good fit of the windows when the hood was raised. As with every volume-produced car, there would be the occasional sieve, but such problems were usually speedily overcome. The Spider was unusual in having a quarter-light window which increased the wind-protection with the hood down, and could provide extra ventilation with it up

Above

The shape of Alfa's renowned, shield-like grille follows on from that of the Giulietta/Giulia, but is low down under the front line of the car and raked back at the base. It was variously described as 'discreet' and 'an afterthought' but started a trend that would endure throughout the Spider series

Above
The attention to detail on the Spider is impressive. The perfectly round filler cap is fitted with a small chromed lip for ease of opening

Right and overleaf
The boat-tailed Spider's unique shape has ensured it a devoted following which has lasted to the present day. Good examples are highly sought after, and make this the most collectible of all the Spiders. The Motor Sport reviewer described his favourite Spider as 'a classical design in an age of increasing uniformity.'

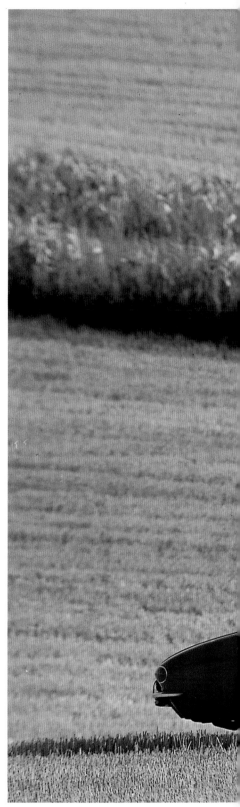

1969, Second Series

The popularity of the boat-tailed shape had grown as the initial shock of the new wore off; the car's balanced style and futuristic profile was being accepted as a classic of design. But Alfa Romeo were not happy with it, so the shape had to change. In 1969, the new shape was presented at the Turin Motor Show; the tail had been chopped, and the second series Spider was underway

The official reason given for the change of shape at the back was the improvement of aerodynamics. As Alfa had never issued official Cd figures for the first series, this was a difficult success to confirm or deny. Journalists who drove the new version at the time found little difference in the 'feel' of the car

Above

No more 'Osso di Seppia'. Of course the new Pininfarina-designed shape was elegant, but the completeness of form was lost. Perhaps following on from such a unique shape, anything else was going to look 'wrong' at least until familiarity caught up with it. The new shape shortened the length of the car by 13 cm; one practical advantage, though, was that the capacity of the boot increased considerably. Of necessity, there were also new rectangular rear light clusters, and new rear bumpers

Right

There were small stylistic changes at the front of the car too; the shield was widened, and the number of horizontal bars across it was reduced from five to three. The bumper, air intake and light cluster unit was changed slightly, and the angle of the windscreen was increased too

Above

The seats of the Spider were comfortable, for driving or just for sitting and having a chat with a friend. The material used was Texalfa, an imitation leather, actually like vinyl, which was very hard-wearing and practical to keep clean. It stayed reasonably cool and well-ventilated too

Left

The second series became known as the Kamm-tail after the chief advocate of aerodynamic tail-chopping, even though he had no direct influence on this particular Kamming. Naturally, both the 1750 Spider Veloce version and the 1300 Junior underwent the same treatment

Above

Classic & Sportscar, *for example, advised would-be purchasers of an older Spider to inspect all the chromework, badging and trim, as replacing them with the real thing is expensive if not impossible. The motoring press generally encouraged would-be owners of second-hand Spiders to go ahead; provided bodywork was clean and engine sound, they would not be disappointed*

Right

In June 1971, the new Alfa 2000 range was shown for the first time, including of course a Spider version. The 1962cc engine had a top speed of 195km/h, 5km/h more than the 1750. The main styling difference externally was the new wheels, with open hubs. Inside, there was a new centre console, a redesign of the dash, and the pedals were now attached from above

Above
Something about the Spider made motoring journalists think of their stomachs; maybe it was thoughts of Italy that did it, because 'first impression' reports overflow with gastronomic comparisons. Ravioli? Tiramisu?

Right
Spring 1972 heralded the arrival of a new, but familiar Spider; the 1300 Junior was joined by a more sprightly one - the 1600 Junior. This car was fitted with the same engine as the original Duetto, and its performance figures were identical. The cheaper and slightly more spartan Juniors had no headlamp cowlings, but a chrome rim was fitted around the glass. The 1600s grille 'shield' was slightly modernised too

Friendly rivalry has developed over the years between those whose preference is for the boat-tailed Spider, and those who prefer the Kamm-tail. This is not merely an old-against-new or original-versus-update matter. Both camps are Spider fanatics after all

At the start of 1975, both the 2000 Veloce and the 1600 underwent a slight change in the engine department, both being slightly lower powered than previously. This brought them into line with other Alfas, which made them more economical to produce

Right from their beginnings in 1910, Alfa's brief had always been the production of light, sporting cars for the enthusiast motorist. Despite air raids, industrial strife and near financial disasters – in 1931, for example, the company was owned by a not very promising sounding government agency, the Istituto di Liquidazione – it has carried on doing just that. The Pininfarina designs, with their futuristic lines, had a youthful feel. No wonder the 1966 Spider and its descendants have become a classic

The shape of this door handle - from a Kamm-tailed 1750 - echoes that of the Spider's famous scooped sides

Above

Testing it in 1971, Motor Trend *magazine called the Spider 'Alfa's free spirit. This is the car for the top down on a beautiful day, the wind tangling your hair, making you want to shout with enthusiasm'*

Right

After fourteen years in production, Alfa rationalised the two Spider models which were still being produced; from then on the 1600 Junior Veloce and 2000 Veloce shared the same bodywork, complete with perspex coverings for headlights. Production of the 1300 Junior had come to a halt some three years earlier. In this particular Spider incarnation, the 1600 ceased production in 1981, followed by the 2000 in 1982

1983, 'Aerodinamica'

Above

Although in 1974 there appear to have been no immediate plans to put the 'new shape' Spider into production, the third series 'aerodinamica' Spiders, first introduced at the Geneva Motor Show in 1983, are quite clearly descended from it. The car is more masculine in appearance than the earlier versions, and has a forthright, no nonsense air, but maybe less charm than series one and two

Right

The 1983 Spider was available in two versions; the 2000 and the 1600. Gone for ever were the Perspex headlamp cowlings of old. The Alfa shield was completely reinvented, plain, with the Alfa Romeo badge large and centrally placed. The front spoiler, of metal painted in the body colour, sits under an extended bumper which surrounded the corners as far as the wheel arches. The rubberised rear spoiler was in three sections. Traditional, instantly recognisable Spiderness was still in evidence at the front …

Left

... though not at the rear. As at the front, the bumper wraps around to the wheel arches, and is prominent both because of its size and colour. The rear spoiler edges the top of the boot lid, with two curved sections at each side shielding the rear light clusters. The Alfa Romeo badge is centrally placed on the spoiler

Above

In many ways the third series Spider is rather overshadowed by the older cars; in boat-tailed and kamm-tailed forms, the 'original' had flown the flag for sixteen years. The new shape did attract a following, but it was generally not of the love-at-first-sight kind. Appreciation came most often after a good few miles of togetherness

1990,
Number
Four

The Geneva Motor Show of 1990 was
the venue for the first presentation of
the fourth series Spider. The previous
series had moved away from the original
Duetto styling towards a more angular,
beefy-looking car. Now there was a
return to softer lines, without losing any
of the modern feel or lapsing into
nostalgia

Above

In the late eighties the company of Alfa Romeo was bought out by Fiat. This gave a whole new outlook to the company in general, and a welcome boost to the funds available for development of new models in particular. Rather than continuing incremental changes to the style already on the market, the decision was made to develop a new body style for the Spider. As in the past, this was carried out in conjunction with Pininfarina

Right

The frontal styling of the fourth series is well proportioned and smooth. The wrap around bumper in the body colour avoids looking like an afterthought. The airscoop is sculptured and breaks the bumper line, its own line in turn being broken by the intrusion of the bottom half of the shield; the badge grows from the top line of the shield down into it

Left

The Spider now has a clean line front to back, similar to that of the previous series' Quadrifoglio Verde, but using body-coloured side strips from wheel arch to wheel arch and matching the bumper lines, rather than side skirts. The famous Spider side scoops, which more or less lost their definition towards the rear end on third series cars, are now well defined once more, a happy risorgimento of a well-loved styling accent

Above

Far smoother at the back; compare these lights with the beetling brows of the back end of the third series on page 76. With Fiat in the wings – and the Fiat parts bin to help out in a crisis – not only is the overall styling of a new body possible, the details are also easier to get right. Ever heard the old saying: the French goverment owns Renault, no one knows who owns VW, but Fiat owns Italy?

Left

Production of right-hand drive cars had ceased in 1978, leaving GB drivers in a difficult position. Many enthusiasts were quite prepared to buy left hand drive and put up with the minor inconveniences. However, some right-hand-drive conversions were made, notably by Alfa Romeo Dealers Bell and Colvill

Above

Britain is surely the one place where an efficient hood that can quickly cover the occupants without recourse to exiting the car or resorting to contortions is essential. Perhaps Alfa Romeo felt that the British weather precluded a really good market for the new Spiders. But Spider enthusiasts are a hardy lot, and not easily discouraged

Above

The interior specification of the latest Spider has undergone a few changes; upholstery is beige, with the option of leather seats. There is a greater range of seat adjustment that benefits the taller driver, and the instrumentation has been changed with the intention of bringing all the necessary information into view at one time, (an ergonomic revolution which has been taking place in most new cars for the late 1980s and 1990s)

Left

Undreamed-of features in 1966; electrically operated windows, illuminated cigarette lighter, electrically adjustable door mirrors, tinted windows, power-assisted steering. Options of leather seats and stereo radio cassette player. The Spider of 1990 runs on unleaded fuel too

Left
There are two versions of the fourth series, with 2000cc and 1600cc engines. In addition, there is the 2000 Spider Veloce destined for the US market, which is identical in looks to the European version, save for the indicator repeaters. The biggest improvement under the bonnet is the provision of power steering on all models

Above
The test driver for Motor Trend summed up the 1990 Spider as "fun-to-drive ... rewarding its passengers more with each passing mile. As with the 'real sports cars' of the good old days, this isn't a car you master at one sitting"

The Spider is of course at home in Italy, as Italian as ... well, let's say as Italian as the 1920s Alfa Romeo racing team manager, Enzo Ferrari ... but when it travels abroad it imparts a little of the Italian spirit wherever it goes, particularly if its warm enough to keep the hood down. How many other cars have endured as the Spider has, over three decades? How many have evoked such fierce loyalty from their fans? Actually, production numbers of the Spider have not been huge; only about 120,000 in total

Above

Just as the early Spiders have become classics, so the fourth series cars will be collectible when they are no longer in production. They are undoubtedly better made, and will be less susceptible to rust than their predecessors - if well cared for of course. When in a few decades time 'nineties nostalgia' is all the rage, these Spiders will be remembered as some of the most stylish cars of the age

Left

Buying a new Spider in the nineties might be the last chance there is to get hold of a brand new 25-year-old car, without the need to haul a hulk out of a barn and spend aeons and fortunes restoring it

The Spiders were forerunners as 'sporty' cars, though their true sportscar potential was limited: Alfa's purpose-built GTAs filled that niche. Nevertheless, the Spider was successful in many rallies, particularly in the US

In several respects, the design that started it all, the Super Flow, presented by Pinin Farina in Turin, 1956. The convex wings with concave scoop, one of the hallmarks of the Spider a decade later, are not merely decorative but also give additional strength to the body

Above and overleaf
The Spider took part in many rallies and hillclimbs in Europe and beyond, with a modest degree of success and a great degree of appreciation. This 'racer' is in fact something of a wolf in sheep's clothing, in reality, a technical exercise based around the Spider

Right
Unlike the intriguing 'retro' racer body styling exercise, the engine is standard: the 2.0 with few frills

Above and right

At the risk of being accused of wandering off the subject, these two front ends make for an interesting visual comparison. Above is the Stradiale version of the 33, with 2-litre V8 engine giving 230bhp. Eighteen examples were produced between 1967 and 1969. This one resides at Alfa Romeo's splendid museum at Arese. There is a family resemblance with the car (right) which is often to be seen at Alfa track events, and indeed with all Spiders. This unconventional body started life in unconventional metallic blue, before remembering its roots and changing to conventional Alfa red

The Alfa Romeo script has long been a feature of the marque, as instantly recognisable as the badge. The thirties flyers had worn the name like a signature across their grilles. Attention to detail on the Spider was praised by many reviewers from the very early days, still the case for the fourth series

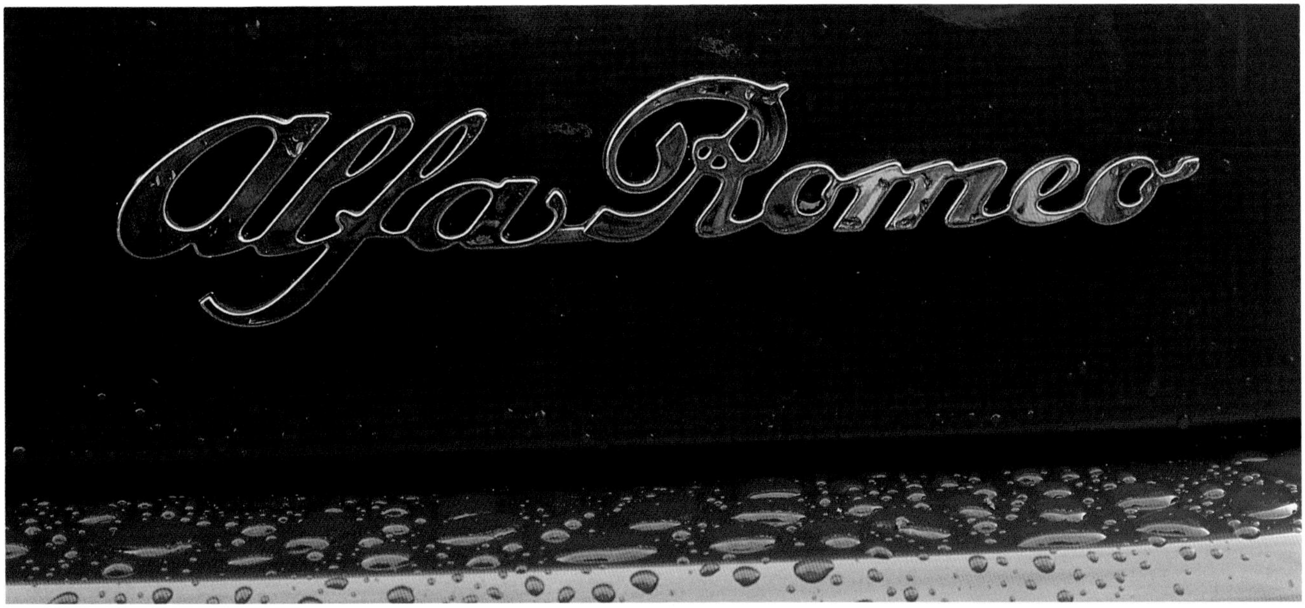
Alfa Romeo

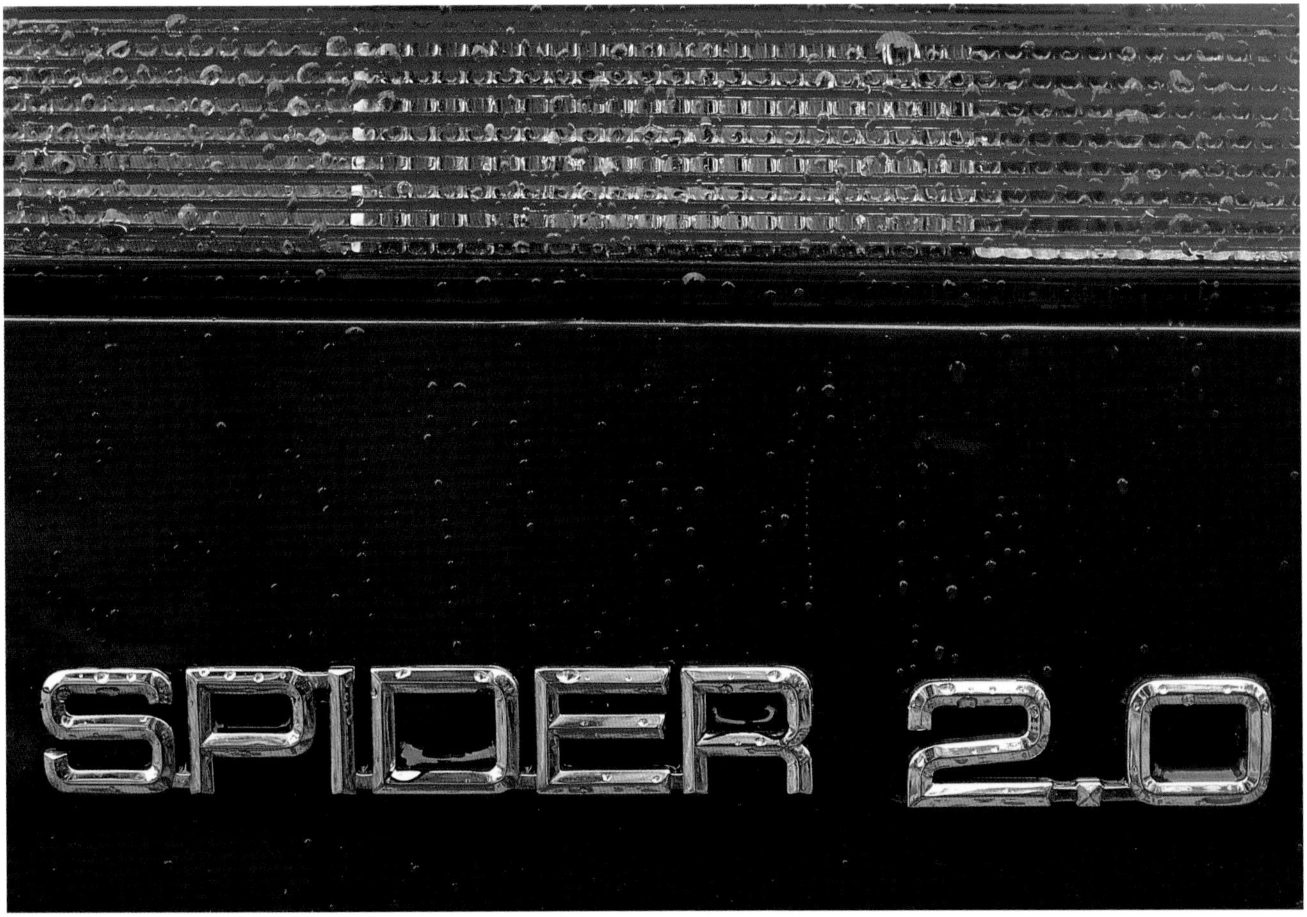
SPIDER 2.0

As with any classic car, spares can be a problem. Specialist suppliers serve the Spider market well with replacement parts, although Perspex headlamp covers are a particular problem. Meticulous restorers will go to great lengths to obtain parts from the relevant, original parts manufacturer in Italy

The newest Spider's removable hardtop; light plastics made removal easy, the unit fitted well. The interior upholstery matches the car nicely. There was an interior light and heated rear window

An earlier hardtop had a slightly more ungainly, unintegrated feel; but there was no escaping the fact that northern European countries would need the protection more than occasionally

Italian-American

Above

*Throughout the years, almost as many Alfa Romeo Spiders have been sold in the
United States of America as in the whole of Europe. Very early on in the Spider story it
was clear that a vigorous American market presence was going to be essential. Italian
culture being a vital, energising part of American culture, and smaller sportscars being
the order of the day across the Atlantic, the stage was set for an export success story*

Left

*And so, shortly after the launch in Europe, three boat-tailed Spiders boarded a boat,
and set sail from Genoa. This was a product launch with a difference; it took the form
of a promotional trip to New York, stopping at Cannes, with American journalists,
celebrities and other influential folk aboard. They were able to drive and be driven in
the cars, and presumably had a little time left over for r & r*

Above

By 1972, the 1750 Veloce was replaced in the US by the 2000 Veloce, which continued in production up to 1982, 26,000 of the two models being imported in total. The major change under the bonnet for the US was the fitting of a fuel injection system. Dual-circuit braking was also a given

Left

Even in the sixties, there was legislation in place in the US to cut down on emissions and improve safety, and these had to be accommodated before any serious US volume sales could be considered. So, in 1968, the US version of the 1750 Veloce was introduced. Kamm tails, and other basic changes in specification, were introduced to the US versions as they came on line in Europe

Above

To conform to US regulations, the Spider has gained indicator repeater lights fore and aft; quite small circular 'pips' on the earlier cars, they have grown to rectangular bars on the later model

Right

American Spiders did not have headlamp cowlings. Instead a chrome ring, wider and more solid-looking than that on the cowl-less European Juniors, provided the finishing touch. The 1750 version had a chrome strip addition across the front of the Alfa grille, while this later 2000 has a one-piece rubber bumper strip which obliterates three-quarters of the shield, and has the Alfa Romeo badge set into it at the centre

Overleaf

Road & Track summing up their test Spider, get quite emotional: "The Spider Veloce is a car that's at home either in town or on the open road. We all envisage such cars on a curvy country road, where little traffic is expected, billboards non-existent, and sunshine and warm air flood you and your companion with the joy of open-air driving"

Above

The rather severe design of the third series, plus the effects of Americanisation, gave rise to some decidedly ugly corners, completely out of tune with the curved style of the earlier cars. Fortunately, the style returned for the fourth series

Right

The rear of the car is very similar to that of the European version, although the injection badge and exhausts give the game away. And although the black trimmings look particularly American, this car lives in England. With the exception of the repeaters, the fourth series Spider of 1990, for the US 1991 model year, bears an even closer resemblance to its European counterpart. Who was in the driving seat? Perhaps it was European tastes in design and style gravitating towards the American

Altogether now

When looking at all four versions together, it is interesting to see how different are the stylings of the sixties, seventies, eighties and nineties, and yet how the characteristic Pininfarina styling shines through. Major changes at the front – Perspex headlamp cowlings disappear on the later cars. The Alfa shield shape evolves as the models change. And the tails of four Spiders? Left to right, third series (aerodynamica), second series (Kamm-tail), first series (Duetto) and the latest fourth series. To each shape its own champion

Above

The next chapter opened on 6 October 1994. At the Paris Mondial de l'Automobile, Alfa Romeo's new Spider was on show for the first time. The design of the car, to be launched in 1995, is the result of collaboration between the manufacturer's Arese Style Centre and Pininfarina. The aim has been to create a car which combines elegance with power, sporty looks with balanced lines. The body is wedge-like, with a tapered front and slightly upward-sweeping tail. It's an approach that does echo a few other recent sportscars, but the upsweep certainly provides a strong identity. There will be two engine versions; a new 1970cc 16 valve 4-cylinder, and a specially developed sports version of Alfa's 2959cc V6

Left

An Italian way of driving - an Italian way of life. The Spider represents the joys of motoring in the open air; a car that must be driven intelligently and well, but rewards the driver who develops the Spider technique to the full

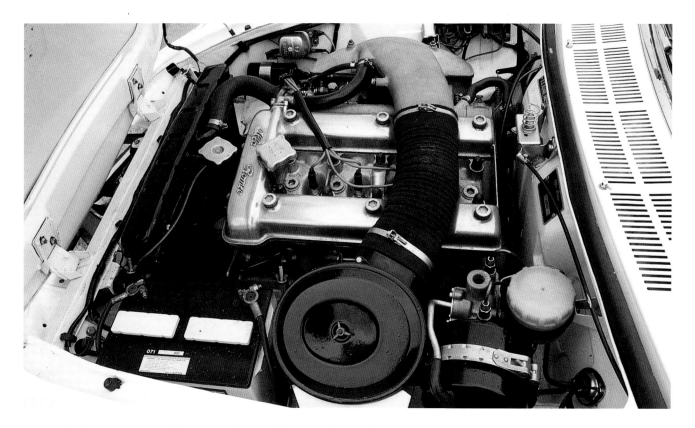

Though the Spider was never about out-and-out performance, these units were more than adequate for the task of shifting the light bodies with sufficient acceleration and speed. 1600 Duetto engine, 1966-68, 109bhp, good enough for standing start kilometre in 33 seconds, for example; the 1971-77 2000 Veloce (pushing a little more weight) in 30.6 seconds. The third engine is the Q. Verde, 1962cc, 128bhp, 1985-89

Specifications

	1600 DUETTO	1750 VELOCE	1300 JUNIOR	2000 VELOCE
DEBUT	3/66	1/68	6/68	6/71
PRODUCTION	1966-68 (from chassis no.660001)	1967-69 (from chassis no.1410001)	1968-69 (from chassis no.1670001)	1971-77 (from chassis no.2460001)
ENGINE/ TRANSMISSION	longitudinally-mounted front engine (gearbox & clutch in-unit). Rear wheel drive	longitudinally-mounted front engine (gearbox & clutch in-unit) Rear wheel drive	longitudinally-mounted front engine (gearbox & clutch in-unit). Rear wheel drive	longitudinally-mounted front engine (gearbox & clutch in-unit). Rear wheel drive
ENGINE	Model 536	Model 548	Model 530	Model 512
Number & layout of cylinders:	4 in-line	4 in-line	4 in-line	4 in-line
Bore and stroke:	78 x 82mm	80 X 88.5 mm	74 x 75mm	84 x 88.5 mm
Cylinder capacity:	1570 cm3	1779 cm3	1290 cm3	1962 cm3
Compression ratio:	9:1	9:1	9:1	9:1
Timing gear:	two overhead valves inclined at 80° in v-formation per cylinder; twin overhead camshafts driven by two chains with a tensioner	two overhead valves inclined in v-formation at 80° per cylinder; twin overhead cam-shafts driven by two chains with a tensioner	two overhead valves inclined in v-formation at 80° per cylinder; twin overhead cam-shafts driven by two chains with a tensioner	two overhead valves inclined in v-formation at 80° per cylinder; twin overhead cam-shafts driven by two chains with a tensioner
Maximum power:	109hp DIN (69.4hp/litre) -125 hp SAE (79.6 hp/litre) at 6000 rpm	118hp DIN (66.3hp/litre) - 135hp SAE (75.8hp/litre) at 5500 rpm	89hp DIN (68.9hp/litre) - 103 hp SAE (79.8hp/litre) at 6000 rpm	130 hp DIN (67 hp/litre) - 150 hp SAE (76 hp/litre) at 6000 rpm
Maximum torque:	14.2 mkg DIN - 15.9 mkg SAE at 2800 rpm	19 mkg at 3000 rpm	14 mkg SAE at 3200 rpm	19 mkg DIN - 21.1 mkg SAE at 3500rpm
Fuel tank capacity:	46 litres (reserve 7 litres)	46 litres (reserve 7)	46 litres (reserve 7)	46 litres (reserve 7)

Coolant capacity:	7.5 litres	9.7 litres	7.5 litres	9.7 litres
Oil capacity:	5.7 kg	6.5 kg	6.5 kg	6.5 kg

TRANSMISSION

Clutch:	dry single-plate	hydraulic dry single-plate	hydraulic dry single-plate	hydraulic dry single-plate
Gearbox:	five-speed all synchromesh & reverse	five-speed all synchromesh & reverse	five-speed all synchromesh & reverse	five-speed all synchromesh & reverse
Gear ratios:	3.304:1 in first, 1.988:1 in second, 1.355:1 in third ,1:1 in fourth, 0.791:1 in 0.791:1 in fifth, 3.01:1 in reverse	3.304:1 in first, 1.988:1 in second, 1.355:1 in third, 1:1 in fourth, 0.791:1 in fifth, 3.01:1 in reverse	3.304:1 in first, 1.988:1 in second, 1.355:1 in third, 1:1 in fourth, 0.860:1 in fifth, 3.01:1 in reverse	3.304:1 in first, 1.988:1 in second, 1.355:1 in third, 1:1 in fourth, 0.79:1 in fifth, 3.01:1 in in reverse
Gear shift:	centrally mounted lever	centrally mounted lever	centrally mounted lever	centrally mounted lever
Drive shaft:	divided	divided	divided	divided
Final drive:	hypoid bevel gear	hypoid bevel gear	hypoid bevel gear	ZF limited slip differential and hyphoid
Final drive ratio:	9/41 = 4.555:1	10/43 = 4.300:1	9/41 = 4.555:1	10/41 = 4.100:1

CHASSIS AND BODY

Type:	two-seater spider (design & production by Pininfarina)	two-seater spider (design & prod. Pininfarina)	two -seater spider (design & prod. Pininfarina)	two-seater (design & production by Pininfarina)
Structure:	monocoque	monocoque	monocoque	monocoque
Wheelbase:	2250 mm	2250 mm	2250 mm	2250 mm
Track	front 1310 mm rear 1270 mm	front 1324 mm rear 1274 mm	front 1324mm rear 1274 mm	front 1324 mm rear 1274 mm
Length:	4250 mm	4250 mm	4250 mm	4120mm
Width:	1630 mm	1630 mm	1630 mm	1630 mm

Height:	1290 mm	1290 mm	1290 mm	1290 mm
Minimum ground clearance:	120 mm	120 mm	120m	120 mm
Suspension:	front, independent with wishbones, coil springs, hydraulic dampers and an anti-roll bar. Rear, live axle with radius arms, central axle bracket location coil springs & hydraulic dampers	front, independent with wishbones, coil springs, hydraulic-dampers & an anti-roll bar. Rear, live axle with radius arms, central axle bracket location coilsprings & hydraulic dampers	front independent with wishbones, coil springs, hydraulic dampers and an anti-roll bar. Rear, live axle with radius arms, central axle, bracket location, coil springs, hydraulic dampers & an anti-roll bar	front independent with wishbones, coil, springs, hydraulic dampers & an anti-roll bar. Rear, live axle with radius arms, central axle bracket location, coil springs, hydraulic dampers and an anti-roll bar
Tyres:	155 SR 15 (Pirelli Cinturato S or Michelin XA)	165 HR 14 (Pirelli Cinturo or Michelin XAS)	155 SR 15, or 165 SR 14 on request (Ceat Drive D2, Continental Pirelli Cinturato RS or Michelin ZX)	165 HR 14 (Ceat D2, Continental Conti TT 714 Firestone Cavallino Sport 200, Pirelli Cinturato HR or Michelin XAS
Brakes:	four-wheel discs. Brake servo on request	four-wheel discs. Servo-assisted with a pressure regulator mounted on rear	four-wheel discs	four-wheel discs. Servo Lockheed Bonaldi, dual circuit with pressure regulator unit on the back axle
Steering:	Burman recirculating ball, or ZF worn and roller	Burman recirculating ball, or ZF worm and roller	Burman recirculating ball, or ZF worm and roller	Burman recirculating ball, or ZF worm an roller
Turning circle:	10.5m	10.5m	10.5m	10.5 m
Electrical system:	12 volts	12 volts	12 volts	12 volts
Dynamo:	300w	420 w	300 w	420 w
Battery:	40 Ah	50 Ah	50 Ah	50 or 60 Ah
Weight:	kerb 990 kg laden 1200 kg	kerb 1040 kg laden 1250 kg	kerb 990 kg laden 1200 kg	kerb 1040 kg laden 1380 kg

PERFORMANCE

Maximum speed:	over 185 km/h	190 km/h	over 170 km/h	over 195 km/h